Exactly W
Are Respo

... Real Es-
tate That a Loved One Leaves
Behind

The Seven Truths About Probate
And
Having the Right Seats Filled on the Bus
for Less Stress ... More Success!

Charlotte J. Volsch

For help with your probate situation, please call, text, or email Charlotte at
760-912-8905 or
charlotte@volschteam.com

Here's What's Inside...

Introduction

I was 28 when my dad lost his battle with stomach cancer. At the time, I lived in California half way across the country from him where I was working on my masters. I borrowed money from a friend to fly back for the funeral. My head was full processing his death, my family, my work, my schooling, and a new boyfriend.

Fourteen years later, my mother lost her battle with Alzheimer's and I lost her completely. It was a very empty hollow feeling after watching and hearing her slip away bit by bit for 3 years from the time she was diagnosed. I was older than when my dad passed. I had more experience with life. I had more experience with death and I had helped coach several hundred families with some best next steps in the care of family members with Alzheimer's.

Life to me is a journey that is not full unless I pass on the jewels of wisdom I learn along the way to help those I meet on their journey along their way. Because of that, I have expanded my reach of help, developed my skills of help and allowed many the space during their times of loss to grieve while I help with many details.

This book about exactly what to do when you are responsible for the real estate that a loved one leaves behind and the truths around that was written because Joe, my dear friend, coach and mentor, suggested I share my truths in writing to help even more, those who find themselves on assignment with a responsibility they feel uncomfortable taking care of.

Sharing my experience as a real estate broker, as well as, the individual stories of some of the executors and administrators (personal representative or PR) that chose to trust me to help them is what this book is all about. We will begin with the first topic, understanding timelines.

Understanding Timelines

The first thing to consider when becoming involved in a probate is being aware of the probate court timelines. If the probate has no unusual situations, experience shows that it can be concluded within nine to twelve months. That time period includes the four-month creditor claims period, as well as, the time needed once your attorney files a petition to actually be heard by the probate court. The hearing is usually within three or four weeks after the petition is filed. Again, your attorney will be informing you of certain timelines, including the important four-month period where any creditor claims would need to be addressed. Your attorney will handle the actual posting of the advertising in a local newspaper and that starts the timeline for the four-month creditor period.

There are certain timelines for the actual probate including the time that you have been given by the probate court to represent the estate (see fig 1.). Your Letters of Administration, some people refer to them as Letters of Testamentary, will have the expiration date of your appointment as executor or administrator. The time before the expiration date is the period of time that the estate is supposed to be addressed and handled by you. It's important to know that those letters have an expiration date, and if they do expire, your attorney will need to go back to the probate court and request an extension for your Letters of Administration. This step involves taking more time and causing additional expenses.

Another thing to take into consideration is the Notice of Proposed Action, also known as the NOPA (see fig 2.). This notice is a document that your attorney will draft when there's some type of an action that's going to occur, such as the sale of the decedent's home. Your attorney will use the document to notify all the beneficiaries. It informs the beneficiaries that you, as the estate representative, will be taking some type of an action that affects the estate. The NOPA, once mailed to all of the beneficiaries, expires after fifteen days. When all the beneficiaries do not object to the proposed action during the time allotted, then you are safe to go forward with the action. Be aware regarding the NOPA that the timeline may be shortened from the fifteen days by requesting the beneficiaries simply check a box that they consent to the action that you're about to take, sign and date the NOPA, and send it back to the attorney.

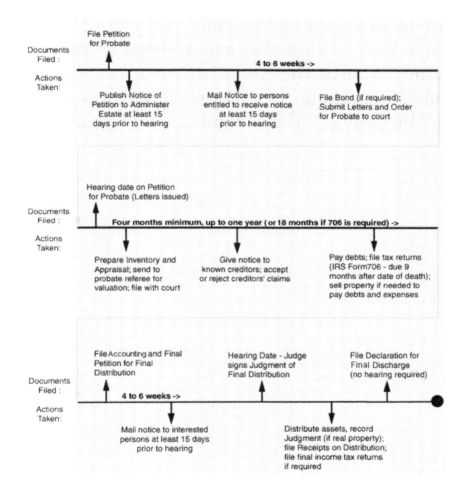

Diagram 1

Because the timelines are so important, it is necessary to have an experienced attorney to assist you through them. Most executors and administrators choose to have an experienced probate attorney help direct them and guide them through all the many steps that need to be taken to properly move through what has to occur in order to successfully complete the probate. Your skilled and experienced probate attorney knows the steps to be taken because that's something they do on a regular basis and will be your guide through the entire process.

DE-165

ATTORNEY OR PARTY WITHOUT ATTORNEY *(Name, state bar number, and address)*:	TELEPHONE AND FAX NOS.:	FOR COURT USE ONLY

ATTORNEY FOR *(Name)*:

SUPERIOR COURT OF CALIFORNIA, COUNTY OF
STREET ADDRESS:
MAILING ADDRESS:
CITY AND ZIP CODE:
BRANCH NAME:

ESTATE OF *(Name)*:

DECEDENT

NOTICE OF PROPOSED ACTION
Independent Administration of Estates Act
☐ Objection ☐ Consent

CASE NUMBER:

NOTICE: If you do not object in writing or obtain a court order preventing the action proposed below, you will be treated as if you consented to the proposed action and you may not object after the proposed action has been taken. If you object, the personal representative may take the proposed action only under court supervision. An objection form is on the reverse. If you wish to object, you may use the form or prepare your own written objection.

1. The personal representative (executor or administrator) of the estate of the deceased is *(names)*:

2. The personal representative has authority to administer the estate without court supervision under the Independent Administration of Estates Act (Prob. Code, § 10400 et seq.).
   a. ☐ with **full authority** under the act.
   b. ☐ with **limited authority** under the act (there is no authority, without court supervision, to (1) sell or exchange real property or (2) grant an option to purchase real property or (3) borrow money with the loan secured by an encumbrance upon real property).

3. **On or after** *(date)*: [_____] , the personal representative will take the following action without court supervision *(describe in specific terms here or in Attachment 3)*:
   ☐ The proposed action is described in an attachment labeled Attachment 3.

4. ☐ **Real property transaction** *(Check this box and complete item 4b if the proposed action involves a sale or exchange or a grant of an option to purchase real property.)*
   a. The material terms of the transaction are specified in item 3, including any sale price and the amount of or method of calculating any commission or compensation to an agent or broker.
   b. $ _____ is the value of the subject property in the probate inventory. ☐ No inventory yet.

NOTICE: A sale of real property without court supervision means that the sale will NOT be presented to the court for confirmation at a hearing at which higher bids for the property may be presented and the property sold to the highest bidder.

(Continued on reverse)

Form Approved by the Judicial Council of California DE-165 [Rev. January 1, 1998]	**NOTICE OF PROPOSED ACTION** Objection—Consent (Probate)	Probate Code, § 10580 et seq.

ESTATE OF *(Name):*	CASE NUMBER:
DECEDENT	

5. **If you OBJECT to the proposed action**

    a. **Sign** the objection form below and deliver or mail it to the personal representative at the following address *(specify name and address):*

       OR

    b. **Send** your own written objection to the address in item 5a. *(Be sure to identify the proposed action and state that you object to it.)*
       OR

    c. **Apply** to the court for an order preventing the personal representative from taking the proposed action without court supervision.

    d. **NOTE:** Your written objection or the court order must be received by the personal representative before the date in the box in item 3, or before the proposed action is taken, whichever is later. If you object, the personal representative may take the proposed action only under court supervision.

6. **If you APPROVE the proposed action**, you may sign the consent form below and return it to the address in item 5a. If you do not object in writing or obtain a court order, you will be treated as if you consented to the proposed action.

7. **If you need more INFORMATION, call** *(name):*
                   (telephone):

Date:

▶

      (TYPE OR PRINT NAME)   (SIGNATURE OF PERSONAL REPRESENTATIVE OR ATTORNEY)

OBJECTION TO PROPOSED ACTION

☐ **I OBJECT** to the action proposed in item 3.

NOTICE: Sign and return this form (both sides) to the address in item 5a. The form must be received before the date in the box in item 3, or before the proposed action is taken, whichever is later. *(You may want to use certified mail, with return receipt requested. Make a copy of this form for your records.)*

Date:

▶

      (TYPE OR PRINT NAME)   (SIGNATURE OF OBJECTOR)

CONSENT TO PROPOSED ACTION

☐ **I CONSENT** to the action proposed in item 3.

NOTICE: You may indicate your *consent* by signing and returning this form (both sides) to the address in item 5a. If you do not object in writing or obtain a court order, you will be treated as if you consented to the proposed action.

Date:

▶

      (TYPE OR PRINT NAME)   (SIGNATURE OF CONSENTER)

DE-165 [Rev. January 1, 1998]   **NOTICE OF PROPOSED ACTION**   Page two
                            Objection—Consent
                              (Probate)

To revisit the mailing of the NOPA, in most cases, that notice is going out to the people, the loved ones, that are connected to the person who has passed away. It's primarily family members or friends, but occasionally there's an entity involved. To touch on that a little bit, sometimes the decedent will leave a will and as part of the will may address that there's an entity as a beneficiary. Experience has been that an entity, some type of a charity similar to the Humane Society or a religious organization, a group that's close to the decedent's heart, is named in the decedent's will. The written will bequeaths a portion of the decedent's estate to this entity. The decedent's beneficiaries do not necessarily have to be family members; friends can be named in a will. With the exception of creditors that's the only way that someone that is not a family member can have some type of a claim on any portion of the decedent's estate.

Most executors and administrators are surprised to learn the length of time to complete the average California probate. They are also surprised that a Notice of Proposed Action (NOPA) is drafted by the probate attorney and mailed to all the beneficiaries once an offer to purchase the home is negotiated. But, they also appreciate that they are protected because of the NOPA, and if any of the beneficiaries would have an objection to the NOPA, the probate court would then need to confirm the sale.

Here's a story about administrator Scott who was also surprised that the probate could take nine months or longer:

Scott's nephew was the only beneficiary and they both thought that once the house sold they would receive the proceeds from the sale quickly. Because they discovered that was not the case, and Scott's nephew was in dire need of funds to pay for a place to live, Scott's probate attorney was able to get permission from the probate court to advance some funds from the decedent's other assets. Scott's nephew received the emergency funds, was able to find housing, and then needed to wait for the remaining proceeds for approximately nine months until the probate was complete. The good news for Scott's nephew was that the decedent had additional assets, as well as, the home.

The Family

Expanding somewhat on the point of family, I'd like to share a little bit about some of the issues or concerns. There are several things to be mindful of, because, as you can imagine, family is a big piece of managing the whole process. When family members and friends have an emotional attachment to the person who is gone, I've witnessed the good, and the not so good. I've seen family members either get along wonderfully with each other and work together towards taking care of all the tasks that need to be addressed to settle the estate. I've also witnessed the flipside when the PR is doing their best to manage an unhappy or uncooperative family member. The difficulty is usually the result of some kind of a family dynamic or because a family member has some issue and will not respect the PR's position of authority. Although having been put into the position of representing the estate, the family member or members can make life more difficult. This makes moving through this process challenging, and not surprisingly it frequently involves the decedents personal property. Sometimes a beneficiary believes that the decedent told them that they could have things, but nothing was written down.

Vincent's Uncle Randy passed away leaving Vincent responsible, as Executor, for his estate. The will read that the personal property and home were to be sold and the proceeds shared with Vincent and his three siblings. Vincent's brother Ralph lived a few miles from their Uncle's home. When the family met to talk about the disposition of the estate, Ralph shared that Uncle Randy had promised that he could have the house and pay the remaining beneficiaries $1,000 per month.

Because Uncle Randy had left a will with specific instructions, Ralph quickly realized that although he believed he was entitled to the home, his Uncle's wishes as written in the will would be adhered to.

To protect themselves and the estate, the PR is put in a position of having to do whatever the probate attorney is recommending. Having a will is helpful because the PR simply follows the decedents wishes as written in the will. When no will is available, the assets including the real estate proceeds are distributed as directed by the probate court. The division of the assets regardless of whatever conversations may have occurred between the decedent and family members or friends will be determined by the probate judge. That is the legal process. Explaining the process to the beneficiaries can be a challenge for the PR. The good news is that most of the time, when beneficiaries understand the process because it has been explained to them, they are cooperative.

The PR is responsible as a kind of overseer of the process. Through their responsibilities in this assignment, it really helps to be connected to a skilled, experienced probate attorney. Because the PR has their own mourning and emotions while they are dealing with the other beneficiaries who may be mostly family, keeping the two separate can be challenging. Having a probate attorney as part of your team gives someone to field questions and perhaps step in and help with the sometimes more extreme issues, also known as the messy stuff.

Susan moved into the home a few weeks prior to her Mother's passing. Her sister, Karen was appointed as Administrator of the estate. Everything seemed to be moving in the right direction until Karen and her brother Steve realized that Susan had no intention of cooperating with the distribution of personal items and the sale of the house. They knew that something needed to be done because the home had a mortgage on it and they were having to pay the monthly payment that Susan refused to pay.

After several months, Karen's probate attorney recommended that she hire a fiduciary to take over her responsibilities as Administrator. The fiduciary quickly realized that Susan would need to be forcibly removed from the home and began the proceedings by hiring a legal group that specialized in evictions. The legal process was followed and eventually Susan was removed from the property by the sheriff. The locks were changed and a temporary alarm system was installed.

Karen was relieved that shortly thereafter the home went on the market; within a few weeks, multiple offers were received, negotiated, and the house sold.

What a relief it can be to have the attorney come along and represent what is to be done according to the law, which protects the PR, and protects the estate. Your attorney is someone to help you by referring to the probate law while handling the disposition of the estate correctly. Additionally, when it gets to situations where family members are doing things outside of what needs to be done, according to the law, your attorney can step in and take action to get things back on track. In some cases, the attorney can relieve you by actually having those conversations with the family including the family member that is not cooperating. The unattached person, the attorney, can be what one of my client's referred to as "the bad guy". The attorney is someone to metaphorically stand behind you and say "well, nevertheless, this is how it has to be". And, the PR can then simply continue with the things that need to be addressed with less tension and uncomfortable feelings.

One last thought I want to touch on is how to keep things as calm as possible by keeping the beneficiaries informed. If the beneficiaries don't know the steps that are being taken, they might get anxious. They may start talking amongst themselves and because they don't have a clear picture, may begin to imagine things that aren't really happening. In most cases keeping the beneficiaries informed does not have to be in the form of any official paperwork, it can just be conversations with them. Communication always alleviates stress for people no matter what process they're going through. When the attorney and the probate real estate professional are keeping the PR informed, then the PR can pass on the accurate information to the beneficiaries. When they know what to expect, and they know what is happening, experience shows that the process goes much smoother.

Because I just mentioned the real estate professional as part of the whole process, I'd like to share a bit about having a skilled, experienced probate real estate professional. A person, like me, who has the right skills, the right experience and knows how to help you with the many details associated with the decedent's home.

It's never too early to partner with the other crucial professional, a real estate broker, that is an expert helping PR's with the decedent's home in probate. The largest asset is typically the home of the decedent including the personal property and proves to be the most time consuming part of representing the estate. Having a professional orchestrator of the real estate process I imagine would be a relief for several reasons. I used the words "professional orchestrator" because my help is very much about orchestrating. My purpose is to provide the answers to your questions, to present your options, to introduce you to people that can help with the personal property and to guide you through the preparation, marketing and successful sale of the decedent's home.

Others, like you, have shared their relief of having someone, like me, to help them make decisions and move forward swiftly.

Another benefit is that the beneficiaries begin to feel comfortable because they see the steps being taken and appreciate the progress. As your probate real estate advisor, at a minimum, you will receive a weekly update that can then be shared with the beneficiaries.

This can be accomplished by including important information about the decedent's home with current facts that can be forwarded easily. Again, helping the beneficiaries to feel calm and trust that everything is going well.

The Real Property and Taxes

The real property, the home, is usually the biggest asset of an estate. Before it is sold, and before the beneficiaries receive their portion of the proceeds, there are some issues that a person needs to consider regarding taxes and the estate.

A question that I'm frequently asked by the PR is, "Is there anything I need to know regarding taxes and the estate?" Because taxes are changing all the time, I always ask the PR if they have a tax professional. A tax professional will be well-versed in current tax laws, and can answer any tax associated questions for the PR. If the PR does not have a tax professional I will gladly recommend and introduce them to someone that can answer questions regarding the proceeds and potential tax liability.

As a wise advisor I know I can't be all things, however, as the orchestrator, I often give introductions to other key players. This has proven to be quite stress reducing for the PR.

The PR should never use personal banking accounts for handling any financial assets of the estate as it can create questions, from the beneficiaries, about how the PR is using the estate funds. To help achieve this, the PR may be instructed by the attorney to obtain a tax ID for the estate. With this new tax ID, bank accounts can be opened to handle any use of funds related to the estate, including the funds from the sale of the decedent's home.

Another important point in regards to taxes is property taxes. Upon the decedents passing the county tax assessor will reassess the property tax to represent the current market value of the house. If all of the beneficiaries happen to be children of the decedent there is a special document called the parent-child exclusion document that can be used. This document can save the estate thousands of dollars, but it is often overlooked. How will it save money for the estate? Much of the time, the home was purchased many years earlier. When the decedent purchased the property they were locked into a lower rate of property tax based on what they paid for the house. Once they passed away, the tax assessor's office reassesses the property taxes based on the current market value. This assessment, in many cases, can mean an increase of hundreds of dollars per month to the property expenses. It often takes six months to a year from the date of death to the date the property closes escrow, which can equate into thousands of dollars in potential savings for the estate if the original tax rate can be kept.

At our Initial Consultation to discuss the steps to prepare, market and sell his mother's house, Bob was surprised to learn that the San Bernardino county tax assessor's office would be adjusting the yearly property taxes from the amount his mother had been paying. He learned that as of her date of death the property taxes would increase substantially from $1,027 per year because the assessor's office reassess the taxes based on what they determine to be the market value of the property. In Bob's case, the current property value was $485,000 and the new yearly property taxes would be increasing to $6,060. I'll do the math for you, the increase is $5,033.00 a whopping $419 per month and if the home is sold six months after Bob's Mom passing, the estate would pay $2,516 to the San Bernardino county tax assessor.

Now the good news is because Bob chose to have me help him prepare, market and sell his mother's house, Bob was pleased to learn that because the beneficiaries are himself and his siblings that the property taxes do not need to increase. I helped Bob to fill out a special document which was submitted to the San Bernardino county assessor's office. This kept the taxes at the amount his mother had been paying, saving the estate thousands of dollars.

The Investors

When I speak with a PR, they often share that they have been inundated with phone calls, and letters from investors looking to offer a quick fix for the sale of the estate property. These investors are trying to convince the PR that they are the best option for an easy sale of the estate with promises of short escrows, and no extra fees. For the personal representative easy equals done! However, these investors have not seen the interior of the house and most of the time not even driven by. Hence, they do not know the condition of the property, and usually are looking to buy at the lowest price possible.

Experience shows, once the investor has viewed the property, they will often make claims about the property such as "oh, I didn't know that it needed a new kitchen, and bathrooms." This is the point where they will negotiate tens of thousands of dollars less than their initial offer. The investors are representing themselves; they are not representing the estate. Which means, any place they can decrease their initial price is a win for them and a huge lose for the estate. They will also offer no extra fees, a misleading deal to say the least, because with all the price cutting they can easily afford to absorb any additional costs such as paying estates closing costs. The investors goal is to entice the PR to take their offer, before they wise up and find a certified probate real estate advisor to represent them.

To prevent investors from taking advantage, the PR should hire a certified probate real estate advisor, like me, who can give them the honest facts about the property value. A probate real estate professional is not trying to buy the property. My purpose is to represent you and the estate, and to negotiate the highest price possible and best terms. There is a saying "negotiating for yourself is like performing surgery on yourself, and you would never do that now would you?"

The PR may have concerns that the cost of a probate real estate professionals commission will cut into the extra funds that they negotiate for the estate. However, this is not the case because the price they negotiate so greatly exceeds the price offered by an investor that it more than covers any commissions. The PR's job is to maximize the amount of money for the estate, and experience shows selling to an investor without representation will surely decrease that value.

Nick was appointed as the administrator for his mother's estate including the home in probate. These are Nick's words: I was contacted by several independent buyers (investors) who were not exactly courteous, they were very persistent and Charlotte, when I hired her, she stepped in and took care of that negotiating process. She was the one who handled all the negotiations, she made it just painless for me. But in the beginning it was somewhat intimidating to deal with investor buyers calling me and yeah, I wouldn't use the term harass, but it was pretty much a very persistent effort to try to purchase my mother's home at a much lower price than it should have been. And, I'm so glad that I hired Charlotte to come in and take care of that aspect of it because if it weren't for her I probably would have ended up selling my property at a much lower price.

Handling all the negotiations with the buyers was the thing that impressed me the most. My mother's home sold for $40,000 more than what the highest offered price by an investor. Charlotte took care of everything and I just simply got a phone call or an email telling me what went down, you know, what happened or what the results were. The probate process can be very intimidating and overwhelming and it was critical, for me, to have a real estate professional who under-

stands the process, who understands what it takes to sell a property in probate. Especially in my case, since my mother's home was at a distance. She made all the difference.

Personal Property

Although the biggest asset of most estates is the house, there is more property to consider. The belongings of the decedent are part of the personal property including furniture, cars, appliances, clothing, jewelry, etc. So what should the PR do with these items? First the PR should partner with their attorney and determine if the beneficiaries will be allowed to remove mementos from the property. Attorneys often want items of value inventoried to be included with the total estate value. However, sometimes there are valuable items that the family members wish to keep and without a will it is up to the PR to determine what may be removed from the estate. During this step the PR should try their best to be considerate as there are often items the beneficiaries wish to keep for sentimental reasons.

Once the family members have removed all desired mementos the remaining property will need to be liquidated. It is important to keep in mind that the personal property may not be worth anything near the amount it was originally purchased for. The PR has three options for liquidating the estate; have an estate sale; sell the entire estate to a buyout company; or donate the remaining items. An estate sale is worth the effort if the estate has a large number of valuable items remaining that can be sold individually by an estate liquidator. Estate sales require a six to eight-week period for marketing and planning. If there is enough time available, this may be a good choice for the estate. Once the estate sale is finished all the remaining items will need to be removed, sold to a buyout company, or donated depending on their condition. The second option the PR may choose is a sell to a buyout company. The company hired to do the buyout will assess all the personal property then give a price they will pay to remove everything. Buyouts are convenient because they will remove all the items including the items that are not saleable. Once a price has been agreed upon, the buyout company will schedule a date, usually less than a week, to clear everything out. This will give the PR an empty property to put on the market quickly. The third option is to donate. When choosing to donate items anything that is small needs to be boxed up prior to having them picked up by the donation company. Someone has to box up all of the items, either the PR, the family members or someone from the outside who is hired to do so. The donation company is then scheduled to come in and remove everything. Like a buyout this option provides the PR with a completely empty property fast, which means getting the house on the market sooner.

Whatever method the PR chooses keeping thorough records of what items are removed at what times is important. The PR should try their best to meet the requirement of record keeping that is established by the probate attorney.

The PR can rest easy when having a probate real estate professional help them handle the personal property of the estate. Many times the PR does not live where the house is located, and they need a trusted real estate advisor, like me, to be their eyes and ears. Having a probate real estate professional to orchestrate how to take care of the personal property will keep the PR from feeling overwhelmed especially if they live out of state.

Carol traveled 1500 miles because she was appointed as the executor of her mother's estate. When she arrived her first scheduled task was to secure the home and all her mother's personal property. The next day her brother and sister met with her at their childhood home. They began the process of going through all the memories and choosing things that were important to them. They soon became overwhelmed with the thought of what was to happen to all the things that they couldn't take to their own homes and turned to me for guidance.

After talking about the three options, 1. estate sale, 2. buyout and 3. donation, the family decided to have me schedule with the buyout company to give them a bid for removing all the things that they left in the home. Because Carol anticipated it would be a lot of physical work, as well as emotional, Carol was relieved that she did not have to pack up all of the things that were left.

Carol agreed to the buyout bid and an appointment was scheduled. Because Carol needed to go home, she gave me permission to give access to the home to the buyout team. Once the remaining personal property was removed, I took photos and emailed them to Carol. She was happy that the next step would be to prepare the home for sale and the home was officially on the market a week later.

Navigating

This brings us to navigating through the entire probate process. Having professionals on the PR's team, dealing with the family, the timing, the taxes, the investors, and the personal property can be exhausting! The first thing is securing and maintaining the property. That can include getting all the utilities transferred into the PR's name, rekeying the property, and possibly having a temporary alarm system installed. A probate real estate professional, like me, can help with all of these details and more with the ultimate outcome of protecting the property. An important step to maintaining the home is to make sure that the property insurance is kept up to date. Sometimes the insurance company becomes aware that the home is vacant and will cancel the property insurance. When that happens, I can help with a referral to a company that will provide vacant house insurance. The next step with almost every home in preparing it for viewings by homebuyers is considering repairs, and then hiring a cleaning company. The probate real estate professional may recommend cost effective repairs, provide an approximate expense for the repairs, and when the PR agrees that it would be a good idea, will help get accurate bids from vendors. The plan would be to have the repairs bring the property up to a point where traditional buyers, rather than an investor, want to submit an offer. Traditional buyers ultimately pay much more than an investor, which is why these repairs may be the best idea. Having the property professionally cleaned will cost between $250-$450 and ultimately make a great impression for traditional home-buyers.

Every probate and each home are unique. Whether the probate property is a fixer and the best scenario is to simply sell as-is or it is determined that with a few cost-effective repairs, fresh paint and new carpet can earn thousands of dollars more, you can feel comfortable when a Certified Probate Real Estate Professional is on your team. Experience is a key component towards preparing the home and ultimately a successful sale.

Jim was named executor in his uncle's will and became responsible for two properties in San Bernardino county.

The largest property located in the Banning area had been his uncle's home. The second house had tenants living in it and provided rental income. At our Initial Consultation we weighed the *benefits of repairs and updates vs. selling as-is. Jim chose to increase the net profit for the estate by improving the property. Spending just over $5,000 on cost-effective repairs including painting most of the interior, hardwood floor repairs, power washing the front porch and a few miscellaneous items proved to be the right decision.*

At the neighborhood open house many compliments were received. The neighbors that had been in the home prior to the decedents passing couldn't believe the transformation. The best news for Jim is that the home sold for 99% of the list price which made the beneficiaries very happy with Jim.

After

When the personal property has been disposed of through one of the three ways mentioned and the real estate sale has been completed, the net proceeds from the real estate sale will be wired directly into the estate account that was discussed in the section under "Real property and taxes". In concert with this step we will also ensure that the closing packet for the sale of the property is delivered to the attorney so that they can proceed in the next step towards closing the probate.

It's important for you to know that in addition to orchestrating the steps through the sale of the property in the estate, I am also here for you as a lifetime resource. Feel comfortable reaching out to me with any questions you may have around the estate, as well as, for any real estate situation outside of the estate. Always think of me as your go-to resource when looking for answers.

Glossary of Common Probate Terms

A

ABATE

To put an end to; nullify

ABATEMENT

Cutting back certain gifts under a will when necessary to create a fund to meet expenses, pay taxes, satisfy debts, or to have enough to take care of other bequests that are given priority under law or under the will.

ABSTRACT OF JUDGMENT

A written summary of a judgment which states how much money the losing party (judgment debtor) owes to the person who won a monetary award (judgment creditor). The abstract is issued by the court so that it can be recorded at the county recorder. The purpose of an abstract of judgment is to create a lien or claim on any real estate owned or later acquired by the debtor located in the county in which the abstract of judgment is recorded.

ACCOUNTING

An act or system of making up or settling accounts; a statement of account, or a debit and credit in financial transactions.

ADEMPTION

The failure of a specific bequest of property because the property is no longer owned by the testator at the time of his death.

AD LITEM

For the suit; for purposes of the suit; pending the suit. (*See guardian ad libitem.*)

ADMINISTRATOR

A person (sometimes a family member) appointed by the court to administrator the estate of a person who died without a will (i.e., a Personal Representative). (See also, *general administrator, public administrator, and special administrator.*)

ADMINISTRATOR WITH WILL ANNEXED

A person appointed by the court to administer the estate of a person who died with a will, but the will either fails to nominate an executor or the named executor is unable to serve.

ADVERSE POSSESSION

The actual, open, and notorious possession of real property, for a continued period of time, held adversely and in denial and in opposition to the title of any other claimant.

AFFIANT

A written statement made under oath.

AFFIDAVIT

A written statement made under oath.

AGE OF MAJORITY

The age when a person acquires all the rights and responsibilities of being an adult. In California, as in most states, the age is 18.

AMENDED

To add to or change a document that has been filed in court by replacing it in its entirety with a new version. In Probate, an Amended Petition will be given a new hearing date.

AMENDMENT

To add to or change a portion of a document

that has been filed in the court by replacing it in its entirety with a new version. In probate, an Amendment to a Petition will not be given a new hearing date.

ANCILLARY ADMINISTRATION

Administration in a state other than the decedent's domicile, when there is also a know administration at the place of domicile.

ANNUITANT
Beneficiary of annuity.

APPEARANCE
The formal act of presenting oneself physically to the jurisdiction of a court; a document identifying representing counsel.

ASSETS
All Property other than income that is part of an estate.

ATTESTATION
The act of witnessing the signing of a document by another, and the signing of the document as a witness. Thus, a will requires both the signature by the person making the will and attestation by at least two witnesses.

ATTESTATION CLAUSE
The clause generally at the end of an instrument wherein the witnesses certify that the instrument has been executed before them, and the manner of the execution of same. A certificate certifying as to the facts and circumstances attending execution of a will.

ATTORNEY-IN-FACT
The individual who is designated in the power of attorney document to act on behalf of another.

B

Beneficiary
An individual or organization to which a gift of property is made. Person (or organization) receiving benefits under a legal instrument such as a will, trust, or life insurance policy. Except when very small estates are involved, beneficiaries of wills only receive their benefits after the will is examined and approved by the probate court. Beneficiaries

of trusts receive their benefits directly as provided in the trust instrument.

BEQUEATH
The first-person legal term used to leave someone personal property in the will, e.g., "I bequeath my car to my brother."

BEQUEST
The legal term used to describe personal property left in a will.

BLOCKED ACCOUNTS
Cash or securities that are placed in a bank, trust company, insured savings and loan or insured brokerage account, subject to withdrawal only upon court order of statute.

BOND
A document guaranteeing that a certain amount of money will be paid to the victim if a person occupying a position of trust does not carry out his legal and ethical responsibilities. If an executor, trustee or guardian who is bonded wrongfully deprives a beneficiary of his/her property, the bonding company will replace it, up the limits of the bond.

BRIEF
A written document that outlines a party's legal arguments in a case.

BYPASS TRUST
A trust into which just enough of a decedent's estate passes, so that the estate can take advantage of the unified credit against federal estate taxes. Also known as credit-shelter trust, A-B trust, or marital life estate trust.

C

CAPACITY
Mental ability to make a rational decision, which includes the ability to perceive and appreciate all relevant facts. Capacity is not necessarily synonymous with sanity. Legal capacity is the attribute of a person who can acquire new rights, or transfer rights, or assume duties according to the mere dictates of his/her will, as manifested in acts, without any restrain or

hindrance arising from his/her status or legal condition.

CASE MANAGEMENT CONFERENCE

A Case Management Conference (CMC) is a hearing between the judge and the parties. A CMC usually happens before a trial is scheduled. Witnesses do not need to attend and evidence is not presented. The main purpose of the hearing is to see if parties are willing to attempt to settle some or all of the issues in dispute before going to trial. If settlement is not likely and parties are unwilling to participate in meditation or a settlement conference, then a Trial Readiness Conference (TRC) and a Trial date may be set. Additionally, Discovery, and Motion cut-off dates are generally given to the parties at the CMC.

CERTIFIED COPY

An official copy of a particular document from a case file that is notated as a true, complete, and authentic representation of the original document.

CHANGE OF VENUE

The transfer of a case from one judicial district to another.

CHATTEL

Any tangible, moveable thing, personal as opposed to real property.

CITATION

A court-issued writ that commands a person to appear at a certain time and place to do something demanded in the writ, or to show cause for not doing so. An order or summons notifying a proposed conservatee of the petition being made, and or commanding the person to appear in court.

CODICIL

An amendment or supplement to an existing will. When admitted to probate, it forms a part of the will.

COMMISSIONER

A person appointed by the court who is given the power to hear and make decisions concerning certain limited legal matters; eg., traffic commissioner, small claims commissioner.

COMMUNITY PROPERTY

Property acquired by a couple during their marriage except by gift or inheritance.

CONFIDENTIAL RECORD

Any information introduced into a court proceeding that is not available to the general public.

CONFLICT OF INTEREST

Refers to a situation when someone, such as a lawyer or public official, has competing professional or personal obligations or personal or financial interests that would make it difficult to fulfill his/her duties fairly.

CONSENT FOR MEDICAL TREATMENT

Power held by conservator of the person only if expressly granted by the court, after noticed motion and consideration of physician's declaration.

CONSERVATEE

A person determined by the court to be unable to protect and manage their own personal care or financial affairs, or both. And, for whom the court has appointed a conservator.

CONSERVATOR

A person or organization appointed by the court to protect and manage the personal care or financial affairs, or both, of a Conservatee. (See LPS conservatorship.)

CONSERVATORSHIP

A court proceeding to appoint a manager for the financial affairs or the personal care of one who is either physically or mentally unable to handle either or both.

CONSERVATORSHIP ESTATE

The conservatee's income and assets.

CONTEMPT OF COURT
An act or omission that obstructs the orderly administration of justice or impairs the dignity, respect or authority of the court. May be demonstrated by behavior which shows intentional disregard of or disobedience of a court order both of which may be punishable by fine or imprisonment.

CONTESTANT
A person who contests the eligibility of a will to be admitted to probate.

CONTESTED
To defend against an adverse claim made in a court by a plaintiff, petitioner or a prosecutor; to challenge a position asserted in a judicial proceeding, as to contest the probate of a will.

CONTINGENT BENEFICIARY
Any person entitled to property under a will in the event one or more prior conditions are satisfied.

COOGAN LAW
In January 1, 2000, changes in California law affirmed that earnings by minors in the entertainment industry are the property of the minor, not their parents. Since a minor cannot legally control their own money, California Law governs their earnings and creates a fiduciary relationship between the parent and the child. This change in California law also requires that 15% of all minors' earnings must be set aside in a blocked trust account commonly known as a Coogan Account.

COSTS
An award of money for expenses in a civil suit or reimbursement for expenses in a probate matter.

COURT INVESTIGATOR
Conducts field investigations and assessments with individuals applying for a guardianship of the estate or conservatorship of the person and/or estate. The investigator interviews involved parties, relatives, attorneys, medical and psychiatric staff, various government agencies, and other concerned parties. The investigator obtains statements, affidavits, and other evidence to prepare detailed reports and make recommendations regarding the suitability of proposed guardian/conservator for judicial review as required under the Probate Code.

CREDITOR
A person (or institution) to whom money is owed.

CREDITOR'S CLAIM
A document wherein a creditor demands payment for debt owed by the descendent.

D

DECEDENT
A person who has died.

DECISION
The judgment rendered by a court after consideration of the facts and legal issues before it.

DECLARATION
A written statement that is unsworn but made under penalty of perjury. All declarations must be dated and signed by the declarant and must show the place of execution and name the state wherein the document was executed or otherwise, that the declaration is made under the laws of the state of California.

DECREE
A court order.

DEED
A written legal document that describes a piece of property and outlines its boundaries. The seller of a property transfers ownership by delivering the deed to the buyer in exchange for an agreed upon sum of money.

DEMURRER
A written response to a lawsuit which, in effect, pleads for dismissal on the point that even if the facts alleged were true, there is no legal basis for a lawsuit. Some

causes of action may be defeated by a demurrer while others may survive. Some demurrers contend that the pleading is unclear or omits an essential element of fact. If the judge finds these errors, he/she will usually sustain the demurrer (state it is valid), but "with leave to amend" in order to allow changes to make the original pleading good.

DEPENDENT
In family law, refers to a person who is financially supported by another person, usually the parent. In juvenile law, refers to a minor who is in the custody of the court because he or she has been abused, neglected, or molested.

DEVELOPMENTAL DISABILITY
Developmental disability is a mental disability that begins before an individual attains age 18, that continues
indefinitely, and that is substantially handicapping. Developmental disabilities include, but are not limited to, intellectual disability (fka mental retardation), cerebral palsy and autism. Handicapping conditions that are solely physical, however, are not developmental disabilities. See "limited conservatorship."

DEVISE
A legal term that now means any real or personal property that is transferred under the terms of a will. Previously, the term only referred to real property.

DEVISEE
A person or entity who receives real or personal property under the terms of a will.

DIRECTIVE TO PHYSICIAN
A document which authorized termination of life support under specified conditions. California's variation of a Living Will.

DISBURSEMENTS
The act of paying out money, commonly from a fund or in settlement of a debt or account payable.

DISCHARGE
The term used to describe the court order releasing the administrator or executor from any further duties regarding the estate being subjected to probate proceedings. This typically occurs when the duties have been completed but can also happen in the middle of the probate proceeding when the executor or administrator wishes to withdraw or is removed.

DISCLAIMER
The repudiation or renunciation of a claim or power vested in a person or which he/she formerly alleged to have. The disavowal, denial, or renunciation of an interest, right, or property imputed to a person or alleged to be his/hers.

DISTRIBUTEE
Someone who receives property from an estate.

DONEE
One who receives a gift. Thus, the beneficiary of a trust is generally referred to as the "done."

DONOR
One who, while alive, gives property to another, in the form of a trust.

DURABLE POWER OF ATTORNEY
A written legal document that lets an individual designate another person to act on his or her behalf, even in the event the individual becomes disabled or incapacitated.

DURABLE POWER OF ATTORNEY FOR HEALTHCARE
A written legal document that allows an individual to designate another person to act on his or her behalf with regard to their healthcare decisions.

E

ELECTIVE SHARE
Refers to probate laws that allow a spouse to take a certain portion of an

estate when the other spouse dies, regardless of what was written in the spouse's will.

ELISOR

When one of the parties is unable or refuses to sign documents necessary to execute a court, the court may appoint the Clerk of the Superior Court or an authorized representative to act as an elisor to sign the documents.

ENCUMBRANCE

Any claim or restriction on a property's title, a debt.

EQUITY

The difference between the fair market value of your real and personal property and the amount you still owe on it, if any.

ERRATA

Errata refers to errors in printing or writing, such as misspellings, omissions, and other typographical errors. It is a means used to merely correct inadvertent errors, not to make substantive changes.

ESCHEAT

A legal doctrine under which property belonging to a deceased person with no heirs passes to the state.

ESCROW

Money or documents, such as deed or title, held by a third party until the conditions of an agreement are met. For instance, pending the completion of a real estate transaction, the deed to the property will be held "in escrow."

ESTATE

A person's total possessions (assets), including money, jewelry, securities, land, etc. These assets are managed by a fiduciary subject to a court order (e.g., guardianship estate, conservatorship estate, or decedent's estate).

EXECUTOR

The person named in a will to carry out the directions as set forth in the will. This person is the personal representative of the decedent's estate.

EXEMPLIFICATION

A formal type of certification in which the Clerk of the Court signs the certification of the document or record. The Presiding Judge then signs attesting to the fact of the identity of the Clerk of the Court, and that the signature is authentic. Finally, a Clerk of the Court signs again, this time attesting to the fact that the judge is a judge of that county's superior court, and that his/her signature is authentic.

EXHIBIT

Any physical object introduced and identified in court and received in a case.

EX PARTE

Latin that means "by or for one party." Refers to situations in which only one party (and not the adversary) appears before a judge.

EXPENSES OF ADMIN- ISTRATION

The expenses incurred by an executor or administrator in carrying out the terms of a will or in administering an estate. These include probate court fees, fees charged by an executor or administrator, attorney's fees, accountant fees, and appraiser's fees.

F

FAIR MARKET VALUE

That price for which an item of property would be purchased by a willing buyer, and sold by a willing seller, both knowing all the facts and neither being under any compulsion to buy or sell.

FIDUCIARY

A person or organization that manages property for a person, with a legal responsibility involving a high standard of care (e.g., conservators, guardians, personal representatives, agents, or trustees).

FIDUCIARY DUTY
An obligation to act in the best interest of another party. For instance, a corporation's board member has a fiduciary duty to the shareholders, a trustee has a fiduciary duty to the trust's beneficiaries, and an attorney has a fiduciary duty to a client.

FINDING
A determination of fact by a judicial officer or jury.

G

GENERAL ADMINISTATOR
One who is appointed to generally administer the entire estate.

GRANTOR
The person who transfers assets into a trust for the benefit of another. (Also known as a "trustor.")

GUARDIAN
A person appointed by the court to protect and manage the personal care or financial affairs, or both, of a minor (ward).

GUARDIAN AD LITEM
Latin for "guardian at law." A person appointed by a court to represent the interests of an incapacitated, mentally handicapped, or minor person in a court case.

GUARDIANSHIP
The office, duty, or authority of a guardian. Also the relation subsisting between guardian and ward.

H

HEIR
A person who would naturally inherit property through a will, or from another who died without leaving a will.

HOLOGRAPHIC WILL
Generally, a will that is completely handwritten, dated and signed by the person making the will.

I

IN FORMA PAUPERIS
From the Latin: "in the way of a pauper." The official waiver of court costs due to the insolvency of a filer.

IN PROPRIA PERSONA (IN PRO PER)
From the Latin: "in one's own proper person." A case heard in which a party represents himself or herself without benefit of any attorney; same as "in pro per." A person who represents himself or herself in a court alone without the help of a lawyer is said to appear in pro per.

INCAPACITY
The lack of ability to act on one's own behalf.

INHERITANCE TAX
California law no longer has a state inheritance tax as such. But if federal estate tax is owed, some of the amount is paid to the state and allowed as a credit on the amount of federal tax owed.

INTERLINEATION
The act of writing between the lines of an instrument.

INTER VIVOS TRUST
A trust set up during the lifetime of a person to distribute money or property to another person or organization (as distinguished from a person who transfers money or property after death).

INTERSTATE
Without a will. Opposite of "testate."

INVENTORY AND APPRAISAL
A list of all assets in the estate at the

beginning of the guardianship, conservatorship, or at the decedent's death. Cash items are valued by the fiduciary; the probate referee values all other items at their fair market value.

IRREVOCABLE LIVING TRUST

A trust created during the maker's lifetime that does not allow the maker or anyone else to change it.

ISSUE

A term generally meaning all natural children and their children down through the generations. Adopted children are considered the issue of their adoptive parents and the children of the adopted children (and so on) are also considered issue. A term often used in place of issue is "lineal descendants."

J

JOINDER

A legal term that refers to the process of joining two or more legal issues together to be heard in one hearing or trial. It is done when the issues or parties involved overlap sufficiently to make the process more efficient or fairer. It helps courts avoid hearing the same facts multiple times or seeing the same parties return to court separately for each of their legal disputes.

JOINT TENANCY WITH RIGHT OF SURVIVORSHIP

Property that names a co-owner on its deed or title. At the death of one of the co-owners the other will become the sole owner of the property, regardless of what may be conveyed in the will.

JUDGMENT

A court's official decision on the matters before it.

JUDICIAL COUNCIL

The Judicial Council of California is the constitutionally mandated body responsible for improving the administration of justice in the state. The council is made up of judges, court executives, attorneys, and legislators. It was established to standardize court administration, practice, and procedure by adopting and enforcing court rules.

JUDICIAL COUNCIL FORMS

The Judicial Council of California has created many forms (called "Judicial Council forms") to standardize the preparation of court documents. People involved in lawsuits (also called "litigants") must use Judicial Council forms that are labeled "mandatory" and may use forms that are labeled "optional."

JUDICIAL OFFICER

An official of the judicial branch of government with authority to decide matters brought before the court. The term "judge" may also refer to all judicial officers, including Supreme Court justices.

JURISDICTION

A court's authority to rule to the questions of law at issue in a dispute, typically determined by geographic location and type of case.

K

KINDRED

All persons described as relatives of the decedent under the California Probate Code.

L

LAPSE

The failure of a gift of property left in a will because when the testator dies the beneficiary is deceased and no alternate has been named. California has a statute (termed an "anti-lapse" statute), which prevents gifts to relatives from lapsing unless the relative has no heirs of his or her own.

LEGACY

An old legal word meaning a transfer of personal property by will. The more common term for this type of transfer is bequest or devise.

LEGATEE
Also known as beneficiary. Person named in a will to received property.

LETTERS
The court document that establishes the authority to act as a guardian, conservator, or personal representative (executor or administrator). In decedent's estates, an executor's letters are designated "letters testamentary," and an administrator's letters are "letters of administration."

LIFE ESTATE
The type of ownership a person possesses in real estate when he/she has only the right of possession for his/her life, and the ownership passes to someone else after his/her death.

LIMITED CONSERVATORSHIP
A type of conservatorship for developmentally-disabled adults.

LIVING TRUST
A trust set up while a person is alive and which remains under the control of that person during the remainder of her life. Also referred to as "inter vivos trusts"

LIVING WILL
Also known as a medical directive or advance directive. A written document that states a person's wishes regarding life-support or other medical treatment in certain circumstances, usually when death is imminent

LODGMENT
A lodgment is a means of submitting documents to the court temporarily. Generally this practice is reserved for a large number of exhibits that have either been deemed too large for the court's file or are needed on a limited basis. Another example of when documents should be lodged rather than filed is in the instance of original documents, such as bank statements, that are submitted in support of a one-time hearing, such as am Accounting.

LPS CONSERVATORSHIP
A specific type of conservatorship, under the Lanternman-Petris-Short (LPS) Act, which allows for involuntary detention and treatment of a person (the conservatee).This conservatorship is a result of mental disorder and the conservatee appears to be a danger to himself/herself or others, or is gravely disabled. (See *conservator* and *conservatee*.)

M

MARITAL DEDUCTION
A deduction allowing for the unlimited transfer of any or all property from one spouse to the other generally free of estate and gift tax.

MINOR
A person under the age of 18. A minor is usually defined as someone who has not yet reached the age of majority. The term does not apply to an emancipated youth. As used in the context of a guardianship, a person under the age of 18 years of age who is placed in the care of a court-appointed guardian.

MOTION
A motion is a formal request made to a judge for an order or judgment. Motions can be filed for any purposes, such as: to continue a trial to a later date, to get modification or clarification of an existing order, for a judgment, for discovery issues, for a rehearing or reconsideration, for sanctions, or for many other purposes. Most motions require the underlying motion to be made in pleading, and a brief of legal reasons for granting the motion (often called "points and authorities"), written notice to the opposing party and a hearing before a judge.

MOTION IN LIMINE
A motion made before a trial begins asking the court to decide whether particular evidence will be admissible. A motion in limine is most often made to exclude evidence by a party who believes that evidence would prejudice the jury or judge against him or her. For example, a defendant in a criminal trial might make a motion in limine to exclude evidence of previous crimes.

N

NET ESTATE
The value of all property owned at death less liabilities.

NEXT OF KIN
The closest living relatives of a decedent, under the California law governing intestate succession.

NOTICE
Information given to a person or entity of some act done, or about to be done.

NUNC PRO TUNC
From the Latin: "*now for then*", used when an order is issued on one date but is effectively retroactively.

NUNCUPATIVE
Oral, not written, form of will – not valid in California.

O

ORDER TO SHOW CAUSE
Court order commanding a person to appear in court at a specific date and time, and to show cause to the court's satisfaction why he or she should not be compelled to perform a certain act (or cease a certain act).

P

PECUNIARY
Monetary; relating to money; financial; consisting of money or that which can be valued as money.

PET STIRPES
By right of representation; made of distribution in which the issue of a deceased devisee collectively take only the share which their parent would have taken if living.

PERSONAL EFFECTS
Belongings of a personal nature, such as clothes and jewelry.

PERSONAL PROPERTY
All items, both tangible and intangible, that are not real property. Anything owned by a person that can be moved such as money, securities, jewelry, etc.

(As opposed to real property e.g., house, land, crops, cabin, etc.)

PERSONAL REPRE-SENTATIVE
The generic title applied to the person who is authorized to act on behalf of the decedent's estate. Almost always, this person is either an administrator or executor appointed by the court to administer a decedent's estate.

PETITION
A written, formal request, properly filed with the court, for a specific action or order. The petition is a pre-printed court form in some cases, or written in proper format on pleading paper in others (e.g., petition for probate, petition for conservatorship, etc.).

Petitioner
One who presents a petition to a court. The person who opposes the prayer of the petition is called the "*respondent.*"

PLEADINGS
In a civil case, the allegations by each party of their claims and defenses.

POINTS AND AUTHORITIES
Also referred to as "P's and A's." Points and authorities refer to the written legal argument given to support a request for a motion. It includes references to past cases, statutes, and other statements of law to give added emphasis to the legality of the motion being requested.

POWER OF ATTORNEY
A written legal document that gives an individual the authority to act for another.

PRAYER
That portion of a petition or complaint that sets forth the requested relief or damages to which the petitioner or plaintiff deems himself/herself entitled.

PREDECEASED SPOUSE

The term applied to a spouse who has died before the decedent while married to him or her.

PRETERMITTED HEIR

A child or spouse who, under certain circumstances, is not mentioned in the will and who the court believes was accidently overlooked by the testator when making his/her will. If the court determines that an heir was pretermitted, that heir is entitled to receive the same share of the estate as he/she would have had the testator died intestate.

PROBATE

The judicial process in which an instrument purporting to be the will of a deceased person is proven to be genuine or not; lawful distribution of the decedent's estate. The legal process of administering a will. Also, the judicially supervised process for marshaling a decedent's assets, paying proper debts, and distributing the remaining assets to the persons or entities entitled to them. An estate may be probated even if there is no will.

PROBATE ESTATE

All the assets owned at death that require some form of legal proceeding before title may be transferred to the proper heirs. Property that passes automatically at death (property in trust, life insurance proceeds, property in a "*pay-on-death*" account or property held in joint tenancy) is not in the probate estate.

PROBATE EXAMINER

The Probate Examiner examines files and documents in pending probate matters set for hearing, providing technical, procedural and legal review to ensure that matters before the court have proper notice and complete documents for a court ruling. The Examiner's work-product is then posted prior to the hearing date for the parties to review and correct deficiencies (or defects) prior to the hearing.

PROBATE REFEREE

An official appointed by the California State Controller to value all property (except for cash type items) in probate, small estate petitions, conservatorship, and guardianship matters filed with the court. Probate Referees also assist trustees in valuing assets in non-probate matters.

PROOF OF SERVICE

The form filed with the court that proves the date on which documents were formally served on a party in a court action.

PRO TEMPORE

From the Latin: "*for the time being*" or "*temporarily,*" a referee or commissioner sitting temporarily and provisionally for a judge; same as *pro tem.*

PUBLIC ADMINISTRATOR

A publicly appointed person who handles the administration of an estate when no other person has been appointed as executor or administrator.

PUBLIC GUARDIAN (PUBLIC CONSERVATOR)

An appointed or elected county officer (and staff) authorized by law to serve as guardian or conservator.

PUBLIC RECORD

A court record available for inspection by the general public. (Compare *confidential record, sealed record.*)

R

REAL PROPERTY

Land and all the things that are attached to it. Anything that is not real property is personal property and personal property is anything that isn't nailed down, dug into or built onto the land. A house is real property, but a dining room set is not.

RECEIPTS

All cash or other assets of the estate received by the fiduciary, other than those listed on the inventory and appraisement. Receipts must be reported to the court on a schedule in the periodic accounting.

REGIONAL CENTER

Private, nonprofit agencies that contract with the state to provide services to persons with developmental disabilities, including assessment, individual program planning, case management, purchase of services, and advocacy. There are 21 regional centers throughout the state.

RESIDUARY ESTATE

Also known as residue of the estate. Portion of the estate left after bequests of specific items of property are made. Often the largest portion.

RESIDUARY LEGATEE

The person or persons named in a will to receive any residue left in an estate after the bequests of specific items are made.

RESPONDENT

The person against whom an appeal is made; the responding party in a dissolution, nullity, adoption, or probate matter.

REVOCABLE LIVING TRUST

A trust created during the maker's lifetime that can be changed. Allows the creator to pass assets on to choose beneficiaries without going through probate.

RIGHT OF SURVIVORSHIP

In a "joint-tenancy" or "community property with right of survivorship," the property automatically goes to the co-owner if the other co-owner dies.

S

SEALED RECORD

A record closed by a court to further inspection by anyone unless further ordered by the court (compare *confidential record, public record*).

SELF-PROVING WILL

A will accompanied by a sworn statement signed by the witnesses under penalty of perjury. Many states accept such wills in order to avoid the cumbersome process of requiring an executor to track down the witnesses.

SPECIAL ADMINISTRATOR

A person appointed to be responsible for a deceased person's property for a limited time during an emergency, such as a challenge to the will or to the qualifications of the named executor. In such cases, the special administrator's duty is to maintain and preserve the estate, not necessarily to take control of the probate process.

SPECIAL IMMIGRANT JUVENILE STATUS

In 1990, Congress enacted federal law to assist certain undocumented children in obtaining lawful permanent residence through a special immigrant visa category known as Special Immigrant Juvenile Status (SIJS). This law helps certain undocumented children in the state juvenile system to become Lawful Permanent Residents. Children involved in adoption or guardianship proceedings who have been abandoned, abused or neglected may be able to obtain Special Immigrant Juvenile Status and, based on that, apply to become a Lawful Permanent Resident.

SPECIAL NEEDS TRUST

A Special Needs Trust enables a person under a physical or mental disability, or an individual with a chronic or acquired illness, to have, held in Trust for his or her benefit, an unlimited amount of assets. In a properly-drafted Special Needs Trust, those assets are not considered for purposes of qualification for certain governmental benefits.

SPECIFIC BEQUEST

A specific item, distinguished from all others of the same kind belonging to the testator that is designated in the will as going to a specific beneficiary. If the specific item is no longer in the estate when the decedent dies, the bequest fails and resort cannot be made to other property of the decedent.

SPENDTHRIFT TRUST

A trust designed to keep money out of the hands of creditors. Often established to protects someone who is incapable of managing his or her financial affairs.

STANDING

The legal right to initiate a lawsuit. To posses standing, a person must be sufficiently affected by the matter at hand, and there must be case or controversy that can be resolved by legal action.

STATUTE

Any written law passed by a state or federal legislative body.

STATUTORY WILL

California form will.

STIPULATION

An agreement between parties or their attorneys.

SUA SPONTE

From the Latin: "*of its own will.*" Commonly used when a judge does something not specifically requested by either party in a case.

SUBSTITUTED JUDGMENT

A legal doctrine by which the court may authorize or direct the conservator to take certain actions relating to conservatee's estate. This may include making gifts or transferring assets to trusts.

SUCCESSOR FIDUCIARY

The next person, or organization, appointed as when a vacancy arises in a conservatorship, guardianship, or decedent's estate because of the fiduciary's death, removal, or resignation.

SUPPLEMENT

Something added to complete a thing, make up for a deficiency, or extend or strengthen the whole. In Probate, these are generally filed to correct defects noted by the Probate Examiner.

SURCHARGE

A money judgment which the court can impose on the fiduciary if the fiduciary's improper acts cause a loss to the estate.

SURETY

One who undertakes to pay money or do any other act in the event that his principal fails therein. One bound with his/her performance of some duty or promise and who is entitled to be indemnified by someone who ought to have paid or performed if payment or performance be enforced against him/her.

SURETY BOND

See *bond.*

SURETY BOND RIDER

A surety bond rider, also called a superseded suretyship rider, is an addendum which the surety attaches to a surety bond in order to lengthen the discovery period beyond the span of time originally indicated in the bond's terms.

T

TANGIBLE PERSONAL PROPERTY

Personal property that takes a tangible form, such as automobiles, furniture and heirlooms. Although such items as stock ownership and copyrights may be represented in the form of paper certificates, the actual property is not in the physical form and therefore
considered intangible personal property.

TAXABLE ESTATE

The fair market value of all assets owned by a decedent at date of death (gross estate) less certain allowable deductions, such as debts of the decedent, last illness and funeral expenses, and expenses, and expenses of administering the decedent's estate (attorney's fees, court costs and newspaper publication fees).

TENANCY IN COMMON

A type of joint ownership that allows a person to sell his share or leave it in a will without the consent of the other owners. If a person dies without a will,
his share goes to his heirs, not to the other owners.

TESTAMENTARY DISPOSITION

A disposition of property in a will.

TESTAMENTARY TRUST

A trust created by the provisions in a will. Typically comes into existence after the writer of the will dies.

TESTATE

A person who has made a will or who has died leaving a valid will; opposite of intestate.

TESTATOR

The person who makes a will.

TITLE

Ownership of property.

TOTTEN TRUST

A bank account in your name for which you name a beneficiary. Upon the death of the named holder of the account, the money transfers automatically to the beneficiary.

TRANSFER AGENT

A representative of a corporation who is authorized to transfer ownership of a corporation's stock from one person to another. An executor or administrator must use a transfer agent when passing title to a decedent's stock to an heir or beneficiary.

TRIAL

In the United States, the trial is the principal method for resolving legal disputes that parties cannot settle by themselves or through less formal methods. The chief purpose of a trial is to secure fair and impartial administration of justice between the parties to the action. To provide a final legal determination of the dispute between the parties. The cornerstone of the legal system in the United States is the jury trial.

However, not all trials are jury trials. A case may also be tried before a judge. This is known as a court trial or a bench trial. A court trial is basically identical to a jury trial, except the judge decides both the facts and the law applicable to the action.

TRIAL READINESS CONFERENCE

A Trial Readiness Conference (TRC) is a hearing scheduled before the trial date. It may be conducted for several reasons: (1) expedite disposition of the case, (2) help the court establish managerial control over the case, (3) discourage wasteful pretrial activities, (4) improve the quality of the trial with thorough preparation and (5) facilitate a settlement of the case.

TRUST

A written legal instrument created by a grantor during his or her lifetime or at death for the benefit of another. Property is given to a trustee to manage for the benefit of a third person. Generally the beneficiary gets interest and dividends on the trust assets for a set number of years. A legal arrangement under which one person or institution (called a "*trustee*") controls property given by another person (termed a "*trustor*", "*grantor*", or "*settler*") for the benefit of a third person (called a "*beneficiary*"). The property itself is sometimes termed the "*corpus*" of trust.

TRUSTEE

The person named in a trust document who will manage the property owned by the trust and distributes any income according to the document. A trustee can be an individual or a corporate fiduciary.

TRUSTOR

The person who transfers assets into a trust for the benefit of another. (Also known as a "*grantor.*")

U

UNIFORM TRANSFERS TO MINORS ACT

California law, which provides a way for someone to give or leave property to a minor by appointing a "custodian" to manage the property for the minor.

V

VENUE
The geographical limits of court's jurisdiction (usually a county, or a division with a county).

VERIFICATION
An oral or written statement that something is true, usually sworn to under oath.

VESTING
Expression of the form of legal title by which property is held. Fiduciaries generally should vest legal title in themselves expressly in their fiduciary capacity. (E.g., "John Smith, as Conservator of the Estate of Bill Jones.")

W

WARD
A person, especially a child, placed by the court under the care of a guardian.

WILL
A legal document directing the disposal of the testator's property after their death. A will is revocable during the maker's lifetime.

WRIT OF EXECUTION
A court order to a sheriff to enforce a judgment by levying on real or personal property of a judgment debtor to obtain funds to satisfy the judgment awarded to the judgment creditor. A Writ of Execution is issued by the court clerk.

WILL CONTEST
A proceeding peculiar to probate for the determination of questions of construction of a will or whether there is or is not a will. Any kind of litigated controversy concerning the eligibility of an instrument to probate as distinguished from validity of the contents of the will. (Will contests are in rem proceedings in that the contest is brought against the thing, the will, as opposed to in personam proceedings, which are brought against a person.)

Disclaimer: The intent of this glossary is to provide the layperson with a general understanding of terms commonly used in Probate Law. The definitions within the document are not comprehensive and are not intended to serve as a substitute for independent research of the law.

Glossary Sourced From:

Superior Court of California

Bio of Charlotte Volsch

Charlotte Volsch is a real estate broker in the Inland Empire in Southern California specializing in probate and trust help since 2012. Charlotte began her chapter in real estate in 1999 bringing to it character traits of ethics, integrity, accountability, responsibility, loyalty, respectfulness, compassion and a humble heart. From her success in corporate America with national recognition, she brought with her skills of organizing, delegating, surrounding herself with those knowledgeable in technology and administration. Charlotte also brings compassion, understanding and empathy from her work in elder care and with the Alzheimer's association

Memberships

CPREA -Certified Probate Real Estate Advisor
PFAC-Affiliate Member of Professional Fiduciary Association of California
SBCBA-Affiliate Member San Bernardino County Bar Association
SRES-Senior Real Estate Specialist
Member of High Desert, Central Regional, California and National Association of REALTORS
Member of Estate Planning Council of San Bernardino County
Member of Estate Planning Council of Riverside County
Member of By Referral Only Advisor

Reviews:

"I've worked with Charlotte on several transactions over the past 4 years and she has been remarkable handling details, meeting timelines and keeping me informed systematically throughout the process." --- Tom Dominick, Esq., Judge Pro Tem

----

"Charlotte and her team are amazing. I had never ever bought or sold real estate and I was terrified of the not knowing the process. I was so relieved to have a professional and empathetic guide with me through the process keeping me informed and making every step easy. I couldn't believe how quickly we were completed ... Administrator Issa B.

"If you are looking for a skilled, knowledgeable real estate broker who knows the California Probate process and the Inland Empire market you need to call Charlotte Volsch. We needed someone we could trust because of our family dynamics. I also needed someone I could rely on because I was out of the area. I contacted Charlotte and after our conversation it was clear that she would sell the house at the best price and terms possible and quickly which is what we needed.

The communication was the best keeping us informed regularly without a missed beat. I so appreciated Charlotte and the team's commitment to the fast-track schedule they had in place for preparing, marketing, and negotiating the sale of mom's house. Such a relief to not have to come to the property during the process and know it was completed so professionally." … Joy L.

"Charlotte is a true professional to and through. I connected her with a client who was administrator for her uncle's estate in the Inland Empire. I needed a real estate broker that was familiar with the probate process to ensure we didn't have any court hiccups due to time delays or incorrect paperwork. I also needed someone skilled with orchestrating property preparation for very little cash from the estate because there was none to work with. Charlotte and her team were amazing. She was able to get the necessary offers to meet the price needed and the 'as is' sale needed, in the time frame needed after preparing the property enough to make it saleable. She has been recommended to my colleagues who have probate and trust cases in the Inland Empire because communication, follow through and knowledge of the process is key." … Bill Francis, Esq.

"Charlotte came recommended to me by my attorney and I'm so glad she was. I was executor of my brother's estate and it was a hostile position due to family. Because I was out of the country most of the time and do not feel comfortable with English, she was able to include a bilingual team member to make sure I understood and was in agreement with any steps taken along the way. Because the property was vacant and in bad repair for a long while she even had her team on a schedule to check the property to keep out squatters or future vandalism. We were able to sell the property quickly at a price I didn't think was possible because of the condition. What a relief when I got the call that it was finished." …Executor Manuel E.

"When mom passed it was so hard for our family and dealing with financial details was almost too hard to put my head around. My attorney recommended Charlotte to come meet with me and help me and the family through the process and I felt like a guardian angel had been sent to us. She was empathetic to our situation and at the same time a true professional at guiding me to what was next every step of the way to make sure we were on track for timelines and moving to a close on this chapter. I am so fortunate to have been sent her to help at this critical and painful time in our lives." …Administrator Jesse D.

"Charlotte and her team were amazing! Being out of state and selling my late father's house was a lot to think about, but right from the beginning, Charlotte was so kind, knowledgeable and responsive! Even after a terrible accident occurred at the house, Charlotte didn't miss a beat in making sure that the property was well looked after and went above the call of duty to ease my mind all the way across the country! Never have I had such a wonderful experience in real estate transactions as I've had with the Volsch Team! Absolutely the BEST to work with!!" …Administrator Dawn J.

References:
Inside a Probate Sale, Gayle Braswell Elison

Nolo Press

Diagram 1, Page 11 "Probate Process Diagram." *Superior Court of California.* County of Alameda, N.D. Wed. 15 Nov. 2016

Dronenburg, Ernest J., Jr. "Claim for Reassessment Exclusion for Transfer Between Parent and Child." (n.d.): 2-3. 14 May 2016. Web 30 Nov. 2016.
https://arcc.sdcounty.ca.gov/Documents/58AHPCEXCL.pdf

"Glossary of Common Probate Terms." (n.d.) 1-17 pag. Superior Court of California – County of San Diego. Wed. 5 Dec. 2016
http://www.sdcourt.ca.gov/pls/portal/docs/PAGE/SDCOURT/PROBATE2/GLOSSARY-PUBLIC.PDF

Judicial Court of California. "Letters (Probate)." DE-/50(1998):pag. 1 Web.30Nov.2016.
http://www.courts.ca.gov/documents/de150.pdf

Judicial Court of California. "Notice of Proposed Action – Objection Consent (Probate)." DE-165 (1998):pag.2 Web. 30 Nov.2016. http://www.courts.ca.gov/documents/ de165.pdf

How to Probate an Estate in California by Julia Nissley

The Typical Probate Timeline: http://www.fasthomehelp.com/blog/2014/06/22/the-typical-probate-timeline-145874

Additional information about Probate – www.inlandempireprobatetrusthelp.com

Made in the USA
Monee, IL
23 January 2022

89643829R00038